What's in this book

This book belongs to

_____

兴趣小组
Extra-curricular activity groups

学习内容 Contents

沟通 Communication

说出学科名称
Say the names of subjects

Extra-curricular activities

Art | Geography | Mathematics | Dance | Music

School Hall and Playground

生词 New words

★ 放学	school is over
★ 一起	together
★ 听	to listen
★ 美术	art
★ 数学	mathematics
★ 上课	to attend a class
★ 作业	school assignment
★ 还有	also
同学	classmate, schoolmate
操场	playground
礼堂	hall, auditorium
地理	geography
知道	to know

还有很多同学在礼堂。

There are also many students in the hall.

这里还有美术小组和数学小组。

There is also the mathematics group and the art group.

调查兴趣喜好并画柱状图

Do a survey on extra-curricular activities and draw a histogram

中西方学校中的活动

School activities in the East and the West

Get ready

1 Does your school have any extra-curricular activity groups?

2 Which activity group do you want to join?

3 Which activity group do you think Hao Hao will join?

fàng xué
放学

yī qǐ
一起

Extra-curricular activity groups →

放学前，大家一起去报名参加兴趣小组。

操场上很热闹，同学们喜欢画画、唱歌、听音乐。

美术小组的人最多，同学们的画很
好看。

玩数学小组的游戏比上课和做作业
更有趣。

礼堂
lǐ táng

地理
dì lǐ

还有
hái yǒu

还有很多同学在礼堂，因为地理小组的电影很好看。

这里有这么多兴趣小组，浩浩不知道怎么选。

Let's think

1 Recall the story. Match the students to their favourite extra-curricular activity groups.

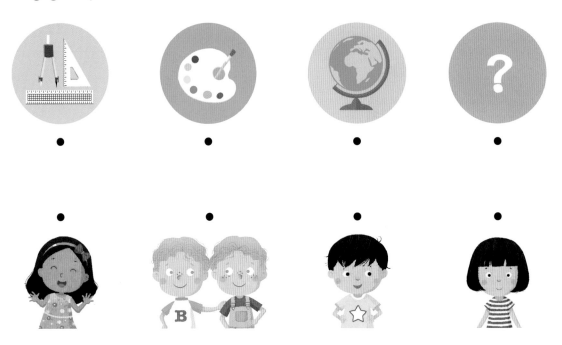

2 Design and draw a badge for your favourite extra-curricular activity group. Tell your friend about it.

New words

1 Learn the new words.

上课

同学

数学

地理

美术

放学

作业

一起

礼堂

知道

操场

听

还有

2 Listen to your teacher and point to the correct words above.

听听说说 Listen and say

1 Listen and circle the correct pictures.

1 上课前，玲玲在哪里？

2 放学后，谁和玲玲在一起？

3 玲玲去了哪个小组？

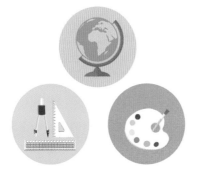

2 Look at the pictures. Listen to the story a

①

放学了，你们去哪里？

我去礼堂看地理电影。

③

我去操场画画，还有几个同学去听音乐。

y.

我们去做好玩的数学作业。

我不知道做什么。

我们一起听音乐吧。

3 Write the letters and say.

> a 作业　　b 数学
> c 还有　　d 美术

我喜欢 ___，因为
我喜欢画画。

我最喜欢 ___。
___英语也很有趣。

放学后，我们一
起做地理 ___。

Task

Paste a photo of your school and talk about it with your friend.

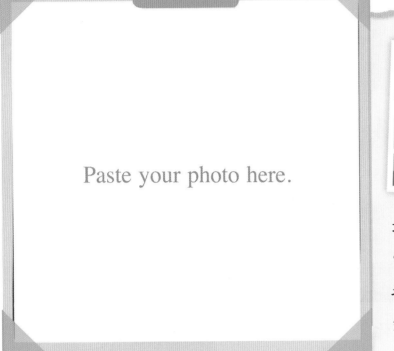

Paste your photo here.

这是我的学校（school）。
学校的操场和礼堂很大。
我在学校学数学、英语、
美术……我喜欢上课。

Game

Look at the picture and circle the correct words. Then read aloud the paragragh.

他是（男孩/女孩）。
他喜欢（地理/
篮球），不喜欢
（美术/唱歌）。还有
他的（数学/英语）
很好。

Chant

🎧 Listen and say.

操场、教室、礼堂，
你去哪里？
美术、地理、数学，
你学什么？

兴趣小组真有趣，
我最喜欢哪一个，
你知道吗？
你知道吗？

生活用语 Daily expressions

一起去吧。
Let's go together.

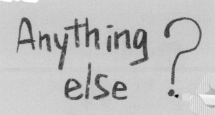

还有什么？
Anything else?

写一写 Write

1 Trace and write the characters.

丶 丆 亍 口 口 叮 听 听

听	听	听	听

丶 丶 ⺌ ⺌ 屵 学 学 学

学	学	学	学

2 Write and say.

他们喜欢＿＿音乐。

这是我的同＿＿。他很喜欢数＿＿。

3 Fill in the blanks with the correct words. Colour the footballs using the same colour.

学　　　听　　　衣　　　跑

放＿＿了，我和同＿＿一起去操场踢足球。我是四号，我的运动＿＿是红色的。球来了，我＿＿八号同＿＿说："快＿＿、快＿＿。"

拼音输入法 Pinyin input

Circle the correct answers for inputting these characters.

a	ai	an	ao	
1 爱	2 艾	3 矮	4 哀	▲▼

ti	tin	tong	ting	
1 听	2 厅	3 停	4 亭	▲▼

ce	kei	ke	ker	
1 课	2 颗	3 壳	4 可	▲▼

We use the 26 letters on the keyboard to input Pinyin. In the Pinyin system, there are 24 vowels including 6 simple vowels and 18 compound vowels.

a o e i u ü

ai ei ui

ao ou iu

ie üe er

an en in un ün

ang eng ing ong

Cultures

There are many interesting activities in schools around the world. Which one do you like?

中国

Radio calisthenics

Radio calisthenics are widely practised in schools. The 20-minute exercises consist of stretching, bending, jumping and other movements.

英国

Rugby

Rugby is a team game. Players can kick, carry and pass the oval ball from hand to hand.

Singing   Austria

Choir is an organized group of singers who sometimes perform in public.

Japan

Kendo

Kendo is a form of fencing with two handed bamboo swords.

美国

Baseball

Baseball is a bat-and-ball game played between two teams who take turns batting and fielding.

Project

1 Find out which extra-curricular activities are popular in your class. Write the numbers.

你喜欢数学，还是喜欢美术？

我喜欢数学。

因为数学作业很有趣。

为什么？

还有吗？

我还喜欢……

2 Draw a histogram to show what activities your classmates like. Tell your classmates about your findings.

同学们喜欢美术小组、数学小组，还有……我喜欢……因为……的活动最有趣。……小组的人最多，有……个。

（人）

数学　音乐　地理　电脑　篮球　跑步　others

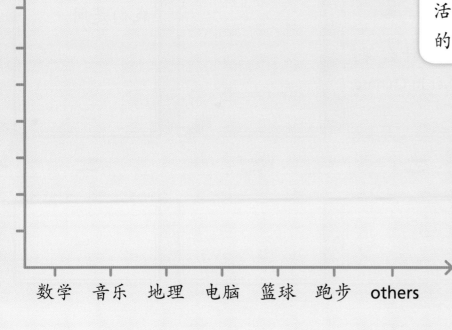

温习 Checkpoint

1 Play with your friend. Complete the tasks in each colour group, then finish the mathematics questions.

28 · Say 'playground' in Chinese.

123 · 我们一起上课。

5 · Does he know? Answer in Chinese.

16 · 放学后，我回家做英语作业，还有数学作业。

+   −   ×   ÷

59 · Say 'There are also many students in the hall.' in Chinese.

94 · 这些是什么课？ Answer in Chinese.

3 · Write 'listen' in Chinese.

4 · Write to complete the sentence. 我们是同

=   =   =   =

2 Work with your friend. Colour the stars and the chillies.

Words	说	读	写
放学	☆	☆	🌶
一起	☆	☆	🌶
听	☆	☆	☆
美术	☆	☆	🌶
数学	☆	☆	🌶
上课	☆	☆	🌶
作业	☆	☆	🌶
还有	☆	☆	🌶
同学	☆	🌶	🌶
操场	☆	🌶	🌶

Words and sentences	说	读	写
礼堂	☆	🌶	🌶
地理	☆	🌶	🌶
知道	☆	🌶	🌶
还有很多同学在礼堂。	☆	🌶	🌶
这里还有美术小组和数学小组。	☆	🌶	🌶

Say the names of subjects	☆

3 What does your teacher say?

My teacher says ...

21

分享 Sharing

Words I remember

放学	fàng xué	school is over
一起	yī qǐ	together
听	tīng	to listen
美术	měi shù	art
数学	shù xué	mathematics
上课	shàng kè	to attend a class
作业	zuò yè	homework
还有	hái yǒu	also
同学	tóng xué	classmate, schoolmate
操场	cāo chǎng	playground
礼堂	lǐ táng	hall, auditorium
地理	dì lǐ	geography
知道	zhī dào	to know

Other words

大家	dà jiā	everybody
兴趣	xìng qù	interest
小组	xiǎo zǔ	group
报名	bào míng	to sign up
参加	cān jiā	to join
热闹	rè nao	lively
音乐	yīn yuè	music
游戏	yóu xì	game
更	gèng	even more
有趣	yǒu qù	interesting
这么	zhè me	so
选	xuǎn	to select
学校	xué xiào	school
吧	ba	(used at the end of a sentence to soften the tone)

OXFORD

UNIVERSITY PRESS

Oxford University Press is a department of the University of Oxford.
It furthers the University's objective of excellence in research, scholarship,
and education by publishing worldwide. Oxford is a registered trade mark of
Oxford University Press in the UK and in certain other countries

Published in Hong Kong by
Oxford University Press (China) Limited
39th Floor, One Kowloon, 1 Wang Yuen Street, Kowloon Bay,
Hong Kong

© Oxford University Press (China) Limited 2017

The moral rights of the author have been asserted

First Edition published in 2017

Illustrated by Anne Lee and Wildman

Photographs for reproduction permitted by Dreamstime.com

China National Publications Import & Export (Group) Corporation is an authorized distributor of
Oxford Elementary Chinese.

Please contact content@cnpiec.com.cn or 86-10-65856782

ISBN: 978-0-19-082251-4

10 9 8 7 6 5 4 3 2